QuEST

Vol 1

Spiritual Thoughts and Talk Starters

By

Jeff Cheney

QuEST

What is a QUEST?

Several years ago, as our children were young, they were assigned to give talks and spiritual thoughts. As we live in a small Branch of The Church of Jesus Christ of Latter-day Saints, this opportunity came very often.

One day our oldest daughter asked my wife what she needed to put into her talk. What she was looking for was the minimum. What did she have to put in to consider it a complete talk.

My wife is one of the brightest people on the face of the earth; she was also an elementary teacher and a seminary teacher at that time, so she was not going to be fooled into giving an easy answer to my daughter. The answer that she gave, however, became a standard in our home and is the basis for this book. She told her that for her talk, and every talk, she needed to have a quote, an experience or story, a scripture and a testimony. We shortened this into Quest.

QU ote

E xperience

S cripture

T estimony

Many years later, we had six missionaries serving from our Branch in many parts of the world. These six included our youngest son, Drew. Because this was such a special time for our Branch, I wanted to do something special for these missionaries. I decided that while they were serving, I would send them a spiritual thought every week in the form of a Quest. As a result, these quests were started.

I have continued to create them and send them, every week, to my nieces and nephews who are serving missions, as well as any missionaries serving from our Branch.

I just thought I would share them with you. I hope they are useful for those times when you need a spiritual thought or a start for a talk.

~Jeff Cheney   2019

Table of Contents

Quest #1
Hope

Quote:
"Thus, real hope is much more than wishful musing. It stiffens, not slackens, the spiritual spine. It is composed, not giddy, eager without being naive, and pleasantly steady without being smug. Hope is realistic anticipation taking the form of determination—a determination not merely to survive but to "endure … well" to the end."
~Neal A. Maxwell   October 1994

Experience:
"I owe much of my happiness in life to a man I never met in mortal life. He was an orphan who became one of my great-grandparents. He left me a priceless heritage of hope. Let me tell you some of the part he played in creating that inheritance for me.

His name was Heinrich Eyring. He was born into great wealth. His father, Edward, had a large estate in Coburg, in what is now Germany. His mother was Viscountess Charlotte Von Blomberg. Her father was the keeper of the lands of the king of Prussia.

Heinrich was Charlotte and Edward's first son. Charlotte died at the age of 31, after the birth of her third child. Edward died soon thereafter, having lost all his property and wealth in a failed investment. He was only 40 years of age. He left three orphaned children.

Heinrich, my great-grandfather, had lost both of his parents and a great worldly inheritance. He was penniless. He recorded in his history that he felt his best hope lay in going to America. Although he had neither family nor friends there, he had a feeling of hope about going to America. He first went to New York City. Later he moved to St. Louis, Missouri.

In St. Louis one of his co-workers was a Latter-day Saint. From him he obtained a copy of a pamphlet written by Elder Parley P. Pratt. He read it and then studied every word he could obtain about the Latter-day Saints. He prayed to know if there really were angels that appeared to men, whether there was a living prophet, and whether he had found a true and revealed religion.

After two months of careful study and prayer, Heinrich had a dream in which he was told he was to be baptized. A man whose name and priesthood I hold in sacred memory, Elder William Brown, was to perform the ordinance. Heinrich was baptized in a pool of rainwater on March 11, 1855, at 7:30 in the morning.

I believe that Heinrich Eyring knew then that what I am teaching you today is true. He knew that the happiness of eternal life comes through family bonds which continue forever. Even when he had so recently found the Lord's plan of happiness, he knew that his hope for eternal joy depended on the free choices of others to follow his example. His hope of eternal happiness depended on people not yet born.

As a part of our family's inheritance of hope, he left a history to his descendants."

~President Henry B. Eyring   April 2014

Scripture:

Wherefore, ye must press forward with a steadfastness in Christ, having a perfect brightness of hope, and a love of God and of all men …, feasting upon the word of Christ, and endure to the end, behold, thus saith the Father: Ye shall have eternal life.

~2 Nephi 31:20

Testimony:

"In my opinion, there has never been in the history of this Church a reason for so much hope for the future of the Church and its members worldwide. I believe and testify that we are moving to a higher level of faith and activity than there ever has been. I pray that each of us will be found holding up our end of the line in this great army of righteousness. Each of us will come before the Holy One of Israel and account for our personal righteousness. We are told that "he employeth no servant there."

There has come with my apostolic calling a sure witness of the life and ministry of the Savior. I declare with Job, "I know that my redeemer liveth." My witness of this "is in heaven." Jesus is the Christ, the Savior of all mankind. Joseph Smith was the inspired Prophet who restored the saving keys, authority, and organization delegated to him under the direction of God the Father and His Son, the Lord Jesus Christ. Of this I testify in the holy name of Jesus Christ, amen."

~President James E. Faust   October 1999

Quest #2
The Work of the Lord

Quote:

"Our faith grows as we anticipate the glorious day of the Savior's return to the earth. The thought of His coming stirs my soul. It will be breathtaking! The scope and grandeur, the vastness and magnificence, will exceed anything mortal eyes have ever seen or experienced."
~Neil L. Andersen   April 2015

Experience:

"My wife, Kathy, and I visited Haiti just two years ago. High on the mountain overlooking Port-au-Prince, we joined with Haitian Saints in commemorating the dedication of the country by then-Elder Thomas S. Monson only 30 years earlier. None of us will ever forget the devastating Haitian earthquake of 2010. With faithful members and a courageous band of missionaries made up almost exclusively of Haitians, the Church in this island nation has continued to grow and strengthen. It lifts my faith to visualize these righteous Saints of God, clothed in white, having the power of the holy priesthood to direct and perform the sacred ordinances in the Lord's house.

Who could imagine a house of the Lord in the beautiful city of Bangkok? Christians are only 1 percent of this principally Buddhist country. As in Haiti we also find in Bangkok that the Lord has gathered the elect of the earth. While there a few months ago, we met Sathit and Juthamas Kaivaivatana and their devoted children. Sathit joined the Church when he was 17 and served a mission in his native land. Later he met Juthamas at the institute, and they were sealed in the Manila Philippines Temple. In 1993 the Kaivaivatanas were hit by a truck whose driver had fallen asleep, and Sathit was paralyzed from his chest down. Their faith has never wavered. Sathit is an admired teacher at the International School Bangkok. He serves as the stake president of the Thailand Bangkok North Stake. We see God's miracles in His wondrous work and in our own personal lives.

The miracle of the Church in the Ivory Coast cannot be told without the names of two couples: Philippe and Annelies Assard and Lucien and Agathe Affoue. They joined the Church as young married couples, one in Germany and one in France. In the 1980s, Philippe and Lucien felt drawn back to their native African country for the purpose of building the kingdom of God. For Sister Assard, who is German, to leave her family and allow Brother Assard to leave his work as an accomplished mechanical engineer required unusual faith. The two couples met each other for the first time in the Ivory Coast and started a Sunday School. That was 30 years ago. There are now eight stakes and 27,000 members in this beautiful African country. The Affoues continue to serve nobly as do the Assards, who recently completed a mission to the Accra Ghana Temple.

Can you see the hand of God moving His work forward? Can you see the hand of God in the lives of the missionaries in Haiti or the Kaivaivatanas in Thailand? Can you see the hand of God in the lives of the Assards and the Affoues? Can you see the hand of God in your own life?"
~Neil L. Andersen   April 2015

Scripture:
For behold, this is my work and my glory—to bring to pass
the immortality and eternal life of man.
~Moses 1:39

Testimony:
"Someday "every knee shall bow, and every tongue confess" that God's ways are just and His plan is perfect. For you and me, let that day be today. Let us proclaim, with Jacob of old, "O how great the plan of our God!"

"Of this I testify in deep gratitude to our Heavenly Father, as I leave you my blessing, in the name of Jesus Christ, amen."
~President Dieter F. Uchtdorf   October 2016

Quest #3
Charity

Quote:

"'Father, where shall I work today?'
And my love flowed warm and free.
Then he pointed out a tiny spot
And said, 'Tend that for me.'
I answered quickly, 'Oh no, not that!
Why, no one would ever see,
No matter how well my work was done.
Not that little place for me.'
And the word he spoke, it was not stern;
He answered me tenderly:
'Ah, little one, search that heart of thine;
Art thou working for them or for me?
'Nazareth was a little place,
And so was Galilee.'"

~Meade MacGuire

Experience:

"Some 23 years ago I was called as a young man to serve as the bishop of a large ward in Salt Lake City. The magnitude of the calling was overwhelming and the responsibility frightening. My inadequacy humbled me. But my Heavenly Father did not leave me to wander in darkness and in silence, uninstructed or uninspired. In his own way he revealed the lessons he would have me learn.

One evening at a late hour my telephone rang. I heard a voice say, "Bishop Monson, this is the hospital calling. Kathleen McKee, a member of your congregation, has just passed away. Our records reveal that she had no next of kin, but your name is listed as the one to be notified in the event of her death. Could you come to the hospital right away?"

Upon arriving there, I was presented with a sealed envelope which contained a key to the modest apartment in which Kathleen McKee had lived. A childless widow 73 years of age, she had enjoyed but few of life's luxuries and possessed scarcely sufficient of its necessities. In the twilight of her life she had become a member of The Church of Jesus Christ of Latter-day Saints. Being a quiet and overly reserved person, little was known about her life.

That same night I entered her tidy basement apartment, turned the light switch, and in a moment discovered a letter written ever so meticulously in Kathleen McKee's own hand. It rested face up on a small table and read:

"Bishop Monson,

"I think I shall not return from the hospital. In the dresser drawer is a small insurance policy which will cover funeral expenses. The furniture may be given to my neighbors.

"In the kitchen are my three precious canaries. Two of them are beautiful, yellow-gold in color, and are perfectly marked. On their cages I have noted the names of friends to whom they are to be given. In the third cage is 'Billie.' He is my favorite. Billie looks a bit scrubby, and his yellow hue is marred by gray on his wings. Will you and your family make a home for him? He isn't the prettiest, but his song is the best."

"In the days that followed, I learned much more about Kathleen McKee. She had befriended many neighbors in need. She had given cheer and comfort almost daily to a cripple who lived down the street. Indeed, she had brightened each life she touched. Kathleen McKee was much like "Billie," her prized yellow canary with gray on its wings. She was not blessed with beauty, gifted with poise, nor honored by posterity. Yet her song helped others to more willingly bear their burdens and more ably shoulder their tasks. She lived the message of the verse:

"Go, gladden the lonely, the dreary;
Go, comfort the weeping, the weary;
Go, scatter kind deeds on your way;
Oh, make the world brighter today!"
~*Deseret Sunday School Songs,* 1909, No. 197

"The world is filled with yellow canaries with gray on their wings. The pity is that so precious few of them have learned to sing. Perhaps the clear notes of proper example have not sounded in their ears or found lodgment in their hearts."
~*President Thomas S. Monson   April 1973*

Scripture:

"Why do ye adorn yourselves with that which hath no life, and yet suffer the hungry, and the needy, and the naked, and the sick and the afflicted to pass by you, and notice them not?"
~*Mormon 8:37–39*

Testimony:

"As Jesus said to the Nephites, so say I today:
"Because of your faith ..., my joy is full.

"And when he had said these words, he wept."
Brothers and sisters, seeing your example, I pledge
anew *my* determination to be better, to be more faithful—more kind and
devoted, more charitable and true as our Father in Heaven is and as so
many of you already are. This I pray in the name of our Great Exemplar in
all things—even the name of the Lord Jesus Christ—amen."
~*Elder Jeffrey R. Holland   October 2010*

Quest #4
Blessings

Quote:

"It is the privilege of every man and woman in this kingdom to enjoy the spirit of prophecy, which is the Spirit of God; and to the faithful it reveals such things as are necessary for their comfort and consolation, and to guide them in their daily duties."
~*President Wilford Woodruff   Deseret News, July 30, 1862, 33*

"The blessings of the priesthood make it possible for every person who is set apart to serve in any office in the Lord's Church to receive "authority, responsibility, and blessings connected with the office.""
~*President Boyd K Packer   October 1994*

Experience:

"A recent nationwide survey found that nearly 8 in 10 Americans "believe that miracles still occur today as [they did] in ancient times." A third of those surveyed said they had "experienced or witnessed a divine healing." Many Latter-day Saints have experienced the power of faith in healing the sick. We also hear examples of this among people of faith in other churches. A Texas newspaperman described such a miracle. When a five-year-old girl breathed with difficulty and became feverish, her parents rushed her to the hospital. By the time she arrived there, her kidneys and lungs had shut down, her fever was 107 degrees, and her body was bright red and covered with purple lesions. The doctors said she was dying of toxic shock syndrome, cause unknown. As word spread to family and friends, God-fearing people began praying for her, and a special prayer service was held in their Protestant congregation in Waco, Texas. Miraculously, she suddenly returned from the brink of death and was released from the hospital in a little over a week. Her grandfather wrote, "She is living proof that God does answer prayers and work miracles.""
~*Elder Dallin H. Oaks   April 2010*

Scripture:

There is a law, irrevocably decreed in heaven before the foundations of this world, upon which all blessings are predicated—
And when we obtain any blessing from God, it is by obedience to that law upon which it is predicated.
~*D&C 130: 20-21*

Testimony:

"I bear witness that such blessings often are significant but subtle. I also declare that the simplicity of the Lord's way that is so evident in the temporal affairs of His Church provides patterns that can guide us as individuals and as families. I pray each of us may learn and benefit from these important lessons, in the sacred name of the Lord Jesus Christ, amen."

~Elder David A. Bednar   October 2013

Quest #5
Feeling the Spirit

Quote:
"We tend to emphasize moments of sublime spiritual understanding. These are precious instances when we know the Holy Ghost has witnessed special spiritual insights to our hearts and minds. We rejoice in these events; they should not be diminished in any way. But for enduring faith and to have the constant companionship of the Spirit, there is no substitute for the individual religious observance that is comparable to physical and mental development."
~Elder Quentin L Cook   April 2017

Experience:
"Once, following a serious illness, I presided at a stake conference. To conserve my energy, I planned to leave the chapel immediately after the priesthood leadership session. However, following the benediction, the Holy Ghost said to me, "Where are you going?" I was inspired to shake hands with everyone as they left the room. As one young elder stepped forward, I was prompted to give him a special message. He was looking down, and I waited for his eyes to come up and meet mine, and I was able to say, "Pray to Heavenly Father, listen to the Holy Ghost, follow the promptings you are given, and all will be well in your life." Later the stake president told me that the young man had just returned early from his mission. The stake president, acting on a clear impression, had promised the young man's father that if he brought his son to the priesthood meeting, Elder Hales would speak with him. Why did I stop to shake everyone's hand? Why did I pause to talk to this special young man? What was the source of my counsel? It's simple: the Holy Ghost."
~Elder Robert D. Hales   April 2016

Scripture:
Verily, verily, I say unto you, I will impart unto you of my Spirit, which shall enlighten your mind, which shall fill your soul with joy;
~D&C 11: 13

Testimony:
"My dear brothers and sisters, old and young, I offer my witness of the glorious existence of the divine beings who constitute the Godhead: God the Father, Jesus Christ, and the Holy Ghost. I bear testimony that one of the privileges we enjoy as Latter-day Saints living in the fulness of times is the gift of the Holy Ghost. I know that the Holy Ghost *does and will* help

you. I also add my special witness of Jesus Christ and His role as our Savior and Redeemer and of God as our Heavenly Father. In the name of Jesus Christ, amen."

~Elder Gary E. Stevenson   April 2017

Quest #6
Adversity

Quote:

"Stick to your task till it sticks to you;

Beginners are many, but enders are few.

Honor, power, place, and praise

Will always come to the one who stays.

Stick to your task till it sticks to you;

Bend at it, sweat at it, smile at it too;

For out of the bend and the sweat and the smile

Will come life's victories, after awhile."

~Author Unknown

Experience:

"I would like to tell you young men of the Aaronic Priesthood a little about my call to a full-time mission. The year was 1962, and a call was received from President David O. McKay to serve in the Mexican Mission. Shortly after receiving the call, I learned that I had bone cancer in my right arm and that the probability of my living many weeks was extremely low. A blessing was received from a wonderful father, wherein he blessed me with my life and that the mission call would be fulfilled, and that I would have a family and be able to serve the Lord all my days.

The doctor congratulated me on being one who had great faith in the Savior but assured me that I didn't realize the seriousness of what I had. As some of you have noticed, I only have one arm as a result of that problem; but ten months after having my arm amputated, I entered the Mexican Mission, full of excitement and ready to work. You see, young men, I had several years earlier committed to the Lord that I would serve a full-time mission and that I would not let anything stop me from fulfilling that call. Well, brethren, the doctor passed away twenty years ago, always amazed to see me still breathing, and he actually became quite interested in the Church.

Brethren, I want you to know that having one arm for nearly thirty years has been one of the greatest blessings of my life. It hasn't been my greatest challenge, but it has been a great teacher to me, teaching me to be more patient and tolerant with others as I have had to learn to be more patient with myself. It has helped me to understand the necessity of our having challenges in life to help develop our character and stamina, helping us to become what the Lord ultimately wants us to become.

~Elder John B. Dickson   October 1992

Scripture:

My son, peace be unto thy soul; thine adversity and thine afflictions shall be but a small moment;

And then, if thou endure it well, God shall exalt thee on high; thou shalt triumph over all thy foes.

~D&C 121: 7-8

And ye shall be hated of all men for my name's sake: but he that shall endure unto the end, the same shall be saved.

~ Mark 13:13

Testimony:

"Your responsibility to endure is uniquely yours. But you are never alone. I testify that the lifting power of the Lord can be yours if you will "come unto Christ" and "be perfected in him." You will "deny yourselves of all ungodliness." And you will "love God with all your might, mind and strength."

The living prophet of the Lord has issued a clarion call: "I invite every one of you," said President Hinckley, "to stand on your feet and with a song in your heart move forward, living the gospel, loving the Lord, and building the kingdom. Together we shall *stay* the course and *keep* the faith."

I pray that each of us may so endure and be lifted up at the last day, in the name of Jesus Christ, amen."

~Elder Neal A. Maxwell   April 1997

Quest #7
Christ

Quote:

"[God] has infinite attention to spare for each one of us. He does not have to deal with us in the mass. You are as much alone with Him as if you were the only being He had ever created. When Christ died, He died for you individually just as much as if you had been the only man [or woman] in the world"

~C S Lewis

Experience:

Although most were doing wonderfully well, a few were struggling with the high expectations of their calling. I remember one missionary telling me, "President, I just don't like people." Several told me they lacked the desire to follow the rather strict missionary rules. I worried and wondered what we could do to change the hearts of those few missionaries who had not yet learned the joy of being obedient.

One day while driving through the beautiful rolling wheat fields on the Washington-Idaho border, I was listening to a recording of the New Testament. As I listened to the familiar account of the rich young man coming to the Savior to ask what he might do to have eternal life, I received an unexpected but profound personal revelation that is now a sacred memory.

After hearing Jesus recite the commandments and the young man reply that he had observed all these since his youth, I listened for the Savior's gentle correction: "One thing thou lackest: ... sell whatsoever thou hast, and ... come, ... follow me."[1] But to my astonishment, I instead heard six words before that part of the verse that I seemed never to have heard or read before. It was as if they had been added to the scriptures. I marveled at the inspired understanding which then unfolded.

What were these six words that had such a profound effect? Listen to see if you can recognize these seemingly ordinary words, not found in the other Gospel accounts but found only in the Gospel of Mark:

"There came one running ... and asked him, Good Master, what shall I do that I may inherit eternal life?

"And Jesus said unto him, ... "Thou knowest the commandments, Do not commit adultery, Do not kill, Do not steal, Do not bear false witness, Defraud not, Honour thy father and mother.

"And he answered ... , Master, all these have I observed from my youth.

"Then Jesus beholding him loved him, and said unto him, One thing thou lackest: go thy way, sell whatsoever thou hast, and give to the poor, and thou shalt have treasure in heaven: and come, take up the cross, and follow me."

"Then Jesus beholding him loved him."

As I heard these words, a vivid image filled my mind of our Lord pausing and *beholding* this young man. *Beholding*—as in looking deeply and penetratingly into his soul, recognizing his goodness and also his potential, as well as discerning his greatest need.

Then the simple words—Jesus *loved him.* He felt an overwhelming love and compassion for this good young man, and *because* of this love and *with* this love, Jesus asked even more of him. I pictured what it must have felt like for this young man to be enveloped by such love even while being asked to do something so supremely hard as selling all he owned and giving it to the poor.

In that moment, I knew it was not just the hearts of some of our missionaries that needed changing. It was my heart as well. The question no longer was "How does a frustrated mission president get a struggling missionary to behave better?" Instead, the question was "How can I be filled with Christlike love so a missionary can feel the love of God through me and desire to change?" How can I *behold* him or her in the same way the Lord beheld the rich young man, seeing them for who they really are and who they can become, rather than just for what they are doing or not doing? How can I be more like the Savior?

"Then Jesus beholding him loved him."

From that time forward, as I sat knee to knee with a young missionary struggling with some aspect of obedience, within my heart I now saw a faithful young man or young woman who had acted on the desire to come on a mission. Then I was able to say with all the feeling like that of a tender parent:- "Elder or Sister, if I didn't love you, I wouldn't care what happens on your mission. But I do love you, and because I love you, I care about who you become. So I invite you to change those things that are hard for you and become who the Lord wants you to be."
~*Elder S. Mark Palmer   April   2017*

Scripture:

"Neither is there salvation in any other: for there is none other name under heaven given among men, whereby we must be saved."
~*Acts 4: 12*

Testimony:

"We solemnly testify that His life, which is central to all human history, neither began in Bethlehem nor concluded on Calvary. He was the Firstborn of the Father, the Only Begotten Son in the flesh, the Redeemer of the world.

He rose from the grave to "become the firstfruits of them that slept". As Risen Lord, He visited among those He had loved in life. He also ministered among His "other sheep" in ancient America. In the modern world, He and His Father appeared to the boy Joseph Smith, ushering in the long-promised "dispensation of the fulness of times".

~*The First Presidency and The Quorum of theTwelve Apostles*
The Living Christ *1 January, 2000*

Quest #8
Resurrection

Quote:

"Through tears and trials, through fears and sorrows, through the heartache and loneliness of losing loved ones, there is assurance that life is everlasting. Our Lord and Savior is the living witness that such is so."
~President Thomas S. Monson   April 2007

Experience:

"One of the Twelve came to me and said, 'Now we would like you to be the speaker at the Sunday night service. It is for Easter Sunday. As an ordained apostle, you are to be a special witness of the mission and resurrection of the Lord and Savior Jesus Christ.' That, I think, was the most startling, the most overwhelming contemplation of all that had happened.

"I locked myself in one of the rooms of the Church Office Building and took out the Bible. I read in the four Gospels, particularly the scriptures pertaining to the death, crucifixion, and resurrection of the Lord, and as I read, I suddenly became aware that something strange was happening. It wasn't just a story I was reading, for it seemed as though the events I was reading about were very real as though I were actually living those experiences. On Sunday night I delivered my humble message and said, 'And now, I, one of the least of the apostles here on the earth today, bear you witness that I too know with all my soul that Jesus is the Savior of the world and that he lived and died and was resurrected for us.'

"I knew because of a special kind of witness that had come to me the preceding week. Then someone asked, 'How do you know? Have you seen?' I can say that more powerful than one's sight is the witness that comes by the power of the Holy Ghost bearing testimony to our spirits that Jesus is the Christ, the Savior of the world."
~President Harold B. Lee   April 1941

Scripture:

"I am the resurrection, and the life: he that believeth in me, though he were dead, yet shall he live."
~John 11: 25

Testimony:

"I bear my witness that the Lord has asked each of us, His disciples, to help bear one another's burdens. We have promised to do it. I bear my testimony that the Lord, through His Atonement and Resurrection, has

broken the power of death. I give my witness that the living Christ sends the Holy Ghost, the Comforter, to those we are pledged to help Him comfort."
~*President Henry B. Eyring   April 2015*

Quest #9
Missionary Work

Quote:
"The Lord made it clear at the very start of this last dispensation that we were to take the gospel to all the world. What He said to the few priesthood holders in 1831 He says to the many now. Whatever our age, capacity, Church calling, or location, we are as one called to the work to help Him in His harvest of souls until He comes again."
~President Henry B. Eyring   April 2013

Experience:
"When I was six years old, Uncle Fred was my worst nightmare. He was our neighbor, and he was always drunk. One of his favorite pastimes was to throw rocks at our home.
Because my mother was a great cook, single adult members from our small branch frequented our home. One day when Uncle Fred was sober, these members befriended him and invited him into our home. This development terrified me. He was no longer just outside but inside our home. This happened a few more times until, finally, they were able to convince Uncle Fred to listen to the missionaries. He accepted the gospel and was baptized. He served a full-time mission, returned with honor, pursued further education, and was married in the temple. He is now a righteous husband, father, and priesthood leader. Watching Uncle Fred today, one would find it difficult to believe that he once brought nightmares into the life of a six-year-old boy. May we always be perceptive to opportunities to share the gospel."
~Elder Michael J. The   October 2007

Scripture:
"Behold, I sent you out to testify and warn the people, and it becometh every man who hath been warned to warn his neighbor."
~D&C 88: 81

Testimony:
"I know that Jesus is the Christ, that His Church and the fulness of His gospel have been restored to earth through a singularly important prophet, Joseph Smith. I testify that devoted full-time missionary service is a source of great happiness and rich blessings, not only for those who

hear the message but also for those who, under the guidance of the Spirit, deliver it. In the name of Jesus Christ, amen."
~*Elder Richard D. Scott   April 2006*

Quest #10
The Rock of Christ

Quote:
"Working toward perfection is not a one-time decision but a process to be pursued throughout one's lifetime."
~*Spencer W. Kimball*

Experience:
"In 1946 I visited Hawaii shortly after a huge tidal wave, where walls of water some forty feet high struck Hilo and the Hamakua coast, and I saw the devastation that resulted. Homes had been overturned and shredded, crushed into splinters like toothpicks; fences and gardens were obliterated; bridges and roads were washed away. Bathtubs, refrigerators, mangled autos lay strewn all about the streets. Where one of our little chapels had stood, nothing remained but the foundation. More than a hundred people lost their lives; as many more were injured; thousands were left homeless. I heard many stories while there of suffering, of heroism, of salvation.

One woman told how she received a telephone message from friends to get out and to leave—that a tidal wave was coming. She looked out to sea and saw the monstrous wave approaching, like a mountain. She and her husband picked up the baby and ran for their lives up the hill. However, two of their little girls were away from home playing near a clump of lauhala trees. They saw the wave coming, ran into the trees, and held tightly with their arms around the tree trunks. The first gigantic wave washed entirely over them, but they held their breath and clung with all their might until the water receded and their heads were again above the water. When the wave receded, they quickly ran up the hill before the succeeding waves came. Together, the family watched from the safety of the hill as their home below disappeared under the pounding of the waves.

We, too, are faced with powerful, destructive forces unleashed by the adversary. Waves of sin, wickedness, immorality, degradation, tyranny, deceitfulness, conspiracy, and dishonesty threaten all of us. They come with great power and speed and will destroy us if we are not watchful.

But a warning is sounded for us. It behooves us to be alert and to listen and flee from the evil for our eternal lives. Without help we cannot stand against it. We must flee to high ground or cling fast to that which can

keep us from being swept away. That to which we must cling for safety is the gospel of Jesus Christ."
~*President Spencer W. Kimball   October 1978*

Scripture:

"And now, my sons, remember, remember that it is upon the rock of our Redeemer, who is Christ, the Son of God, that ye must build your foundation; that when the devil shall send forth his mighty winds, yea, his shafts in the whirlwind, yea, when all his hail and his mighty storm shall beat upon you, it shall have no power over you to drag you down to the gulf of misery and endless wo, because of the rock upon which ye are built, which is a sure foundation, a foundation whereon if men build they cannot fall."
~*Helaman 5:12*

Testimony:

"Brothers and sisters, we are all called to be disciples of our Savior. Let this conference be your opportunity to "begin as in times of old, and come unto [Him] with all your heart. This is His Church. I bear my special witness that He lives. May He bless us in our eternal quest to become devoted and valiant disciples. In the name of Jesus Christ, amen."
~*Elder Robert D. Hales   April 2017*

Quest #11
Temple Work

Quote:

"Many suppose that they are discharging their responsibilities by simply "going to the temple." But that is not wholly true. We must go to the temple, of course, and often. It we do not as yet have the records of our own dead kindred, then while we search for them, by all means let us help others with theirs.

But be it understood that if we go to the temple, and not for our own dead, we are performing only a part of our duty, because we are also required to go there specifically to save our own dead relatives and bind the various generations together by the power of the holy priesthood.

We must disabuse our minds of the idea that merely "going to the temple" discharges our full responsibility, because it does not. That is not enough.

We must get down to specifics and do the work for our own dead progenitors."

~Elder Mark E. Petersen   April 1976

Experience:

"I remember … as a … boy, coming in from the field and approaching the old farm home. … I could hear my mother singing, 'Have I Done Any Good in the World Today?' (Hymns, 1950, no. 58.) I can … see her in my mind's eye bending over the ironing board … with beads of perspiration on her forehead." She was ironing long strips of white cloth, with newspapers on the floor to keep them clean. "When I asked her what she was doing, she said, 'These are temple robes, my son. Your father and I are going to the Logan Temple.'

"Then she put the old flatiron on the stove, drew a chair close to mine, and told me about temple work—how important it [was] to be able to go to the temple and participate in the sacred ordinances performed there. She also expressed her fervent hope that some day her children … grandchildren and great-grandchildren would have the opportunity to enjoy those priceless blessings. I am happy to say that her fondest hopes in large measure have been realized."

~President Ezra Taft Benson

Scripture:

"Behold, I will send you Elijah the prophet before the coming of the great and dreadful day of the Lord:

And he shall turn the heart of the fathers to the children, and the heart of the children to their fathers, lest I come and smite the earth with a curse."
~*Malachi 4: 5-6*

<u>Testimony:</u>

"And now, brothers and sisters, I want to testify concerning this sacred work. I know that it is true. The principles are eternal. The ordinances are divine—they are eternal—framed before the world was. You and I are responsible to carry on this work. The Lord has no one else to do it. Surely this is not an onerous burden! It is a privilege. A temple recommend is one of the highest accolades we may receive. To use it regularly permits us to participate in the choicest gifts within the keeping of the Church. Those who attend feel a special spirit there. Peace comes. I know that their service there assists a departed one to gain exaltation. And I know that they in turn qualify for blessings from the other side of the veil. And I know that blessings will follow you home from the temple. God lives. Jesus is the Christ. This is the consummate work of the kingdom. In the name of Jesus Christ, amen."
~*Elder A. Theodore Tuttle   April 1982*

Quest #12
Love My Neighbor

Quote:

He drew a circle that shut me out—
Heretic, rebel, a thing to flout.
But Love and I had the wit to win:
We drew a circle that took him in!
~Edwin Markham

Experience:

"On a cold winter morning, the street cleaning crew [in Salt Lake City] was removing large chunks of ice from the street gutters. The regular crew was assisted by temporary laborers who desperately needed the work. One such wore only a lightweight sweater and was suffering from the cold. A slender man with a well-groomed beard stopped by the crew and asked the worker, 'You need more than that sweater on a morning like this. Where is your coat?' The man replied that he had no coat to wear. The visitor then removed his own overcoat, handed it to the man and said, 'This coat is yours. It is heavy wool and will keep you warm. I just work across the street.' The street was South Temple. The good Samaritan who walked into the Church Administration Building to his daily work and without his coat was President George Albert Smith of The Church of Jesus Christ of Latter-day Saints. His selfless act of generosity revealed his tender heart. Surely he was his brother's keeper."
~ President Thomas S. Monson

Scripture:

"Thou shalt love the Lord thy God with all thy heart, and with all thy soul, and with all thy mind, this is the first and great commandment.
"And the second is like unto it, Thou shalt love thy neighbor as thyself. On these two commandments hang all the law and the prophets."
~Matthew 22:37–40

Testimony:

"I know this gospel is true. I have no doubt about that at all. I never remember a time when I questioned a principle of the gospel. I know that the welfare program that was outlined in the 1930s was inspired of the Lord. He gave President Grant the inspiration and gave him help through his great counselor, J. Reuben Clark, Jr., and others, to set up the program. It is our duty now to follow it and take care of His kingdom in the spirit of loving our neighbors as ourselves.

If we do so, we shall be able to meet the trying days ahead, which are coming faster than we think. The peoples of the earth will be in such trouble and distress that they will be unable to solve their problems in any other way than to turn to the Lord's program. I bear you this testimony in the name of Jesus Christ. Amen."
~President Marion G. Romney   April 1978

Quest #13
Word of God

Quote:

"Sometimes, the truth may just seem too straightforward, too plain, and too simple for us to fully appreciate its great value. So we set aside what we have experienced and know to be true in pursuit of more mysterious or complicated information. Hopefully we will learn that when we chase after shadows, we are pursuing matters that have little substance and value."

~Dieter F. Uchtdorf

Experience:

"On October 6, in the year 1536, a pitiful figure was led from a dungeon in Vilvorde Castle near Brussels, Belgium. For nearly a year and a half, the man had suffered isolation in a dark, damp cell. Now outside the castle wall, the prisoner was fastened to a post. He had time to utter aloud his final prayer, "Lord! open the king of England's eyes," and then he was strangled. Immediately, his body was burned at the stake. Who was this man, and what was the offense for which both political and ecclesiastical authorities had condemned him? His name was William Tyndale, and his crime was to have translated and published the Bible in English.

Tyndale, born in England about the time Columbus sailed to the new world, was educated at Oxford and Cambridge and then became a member of the Catholic clergy. He was fluent in eight languages, including Greek, Hebrew, and Latin. Tyndale was a devoted student of the Bible, and the pervasive ignorance of the scriptures that he observed in both priests and lay people troubled him deeply. In a heated exchange with a cleric who argued against putting scripture in the hands of the common man, Tyndale vowed, "If God spare my life, ere many years I will cause a boy that driveth the plough, shall know more of the Scripture than thou dost!"

He sought the approval of church authorities to prepare a translation of the Bible in English so that all could read and apply the word of God. It was denied—the prevailing view being that direct access to the scriptures by any but the clergy threatened the authority of the church and was tantamount to casting "pearls before swine" (Matthew 7:6).

Tyndale nevertheless undertook the challenging work of translation. In 1524 he traveled to Germany, under an assumed name, where he lived much of the time in hiding, under constant threat of arrest. With the help of committed friends, Tyndale was able to publish English translations of the New Testament and later the Old Testament. The Bibles were smuggled into England, where they were in great demand and much prized by those who could get them. They were shared widely but in secret. The authorities burned all the copies they could find. Nevertheless, within three years of Tyndale's death, God did indeed open King Henry VIII's eyes, and with publication of what was called the "Great Bible," the scriptures in English began to be publicly available. Tyndale's work became the foundation for almost all future English translations of the Bible, most notably the King James Version.

Scripture:

"Whoso would hearken unto the word of God, and would hold fast unto it, they would never perish; neither could the temptations and the fiery darts of the adversary overpower them unto blindness, to lead them away to destruction."

~1 Nephi 15:24

Testimony:

"May we feast continuously on the words of Christ that will tell us all things we should do (see 2 Nephi 32:3). I have studied the scriptures, I have pondered the scriptures, and on this Eastertide, I bear you my testimony of the Father and the Son, as They are revealed in the holy scriptures, in the name of Jesus Christ, amen."

~Elder D. Todd Christofferson   October 2010

Quest #14
Tender Mercies of the Lord

Quote:

"Every one of us is more beloved to the Lord than we can possibly understand or imagine. Let us therefore be kinder to one another and kinder toward ourselves. Let us remember that as we wait upon the Lord, we are becoming "saint[s] through [His] atonement, ... submissive, meek, humble, patient, full of love, willing to submit to all things which the Lord seeth fit to inflict upon [us], even as a child doth submit to his father."

Such was the submission of our Savior to His Father in the Garden of Gethsemane. He implored His disciples, "Watch with me," yet three times He returned to them to find their eyes heavy with sleep. Without the companionship of these disciples and ultimately without the presence of His Father, the Savior chose to suffer our "pains and afflictions and temptations of every kind." With an angel sent to strengthen Him, He "shrank not to drink the bitter cup." He waited upon His Father, saying, "Thy will be done," and He humbly trod the winepress alone. Now, as one of His Twelve Apostles in these latter days, I pray that we will be strengthened to watch with Him and wait upon Him through all our days."
~Elder Robert D. Hales   October 2011

Experience:

"Six months ago, I stood at this pulpit for the first time as the newest member of the Quorum of the Twelve Apostles. Both then and even more so now, I have felt and feel the weight of the call to serve and of the responsibility to teach with clarity and to testify with authority. I pray for and invite the assistance of the Holy Ghost as I now speak with you. This afternoon I want to describe and discuss a spiritual impression I received a few moments before I stepped to this pulpit during the Sunday morning session of general conference last October. Elder Dieter F. Uchtdorf had just finished speaking and had declared his powerful witness of the Savior. Then we all stood together to sing the intermediate hymn that previously had been announced by President Gordon B. Hinckley. The intermediate hymn that morning was "Redeemer of Israel" (*Hymns*, no. 6).

Now, the music for the various conference sessions had been determined many weeks before—and obviously long before my new call to serve. If, however, I had been invited to suggest an intermediate hymn for that particular session of the conference—a hymn that would have been both edifying and spiritually soothing for me and for the congregation before my first address in this Conference Center—I would have selected my favorite hymn, "Redeemer of Israel." Tears filled my eyes as I stood with you to sing that stirring hymn of the Restoration.

Near the conclusion of the singing, to my mind came this verse from the Book of Mormon: "But behold, I, Nephi, will show unto you that the tender mercies of the Lord are over all those whom he hath chosen, because of their faith, to make them mighty even unto the power of deliverance" (1 Ne. 1:20).

My mind was drawn immediately to Nephi's phrase "the tender mercies of the Lord," and I knew in that very moment I was experiencing just such a tender mercy. A loving Savior was sending me a most personal and timely message of comfort and reassurance through a hymn selected weeks previously. Some may count this experience as simply a nice coincidence, but I testify that the tender mercies of the Lord are real and that they do not occur randomly or merely by coincidence. Often, the Lord's timing of His tender mercies helps us to both discern and acknowledge them."

~Elder David A. Bednar   April 2005

Scripture:

"But behold, I, Nephi, will show unto you that the tender mercies of the Lord are over all those whom he hath chosen, because of their faith, to make them mighty even unto the power of deliverance"

~1 Nephi 1:20

Testimony:

"I know He lives. I know He loves us. I know we can feel His love here and now. I know His voice is one of perfect mildness which penetrates to our very center. I know He smiles and is filled with compassion and love. I know He is full of gentleness, kindness, mercy, and desire to help. I love Him with all my heart. I testify that when we are ready, His pure love instantly moves across time and space, reaches down, and pulls us up from the depths of any tumultuous sea of darkness, sin, sorrow, death, or despair we may find ourselves in and brings us into the light and life and love of eternity. In the name of Jesus Christ, amen."

~Elder John H. Groberg   October 2004

Quest #15
Prayer

Quote:

"There will be noise and people around you most of your waking day. God hears your silent prayers, but you may have to learn to shut out the distractions because the moment you need the connection with God may not come in quiet times."

~President Henry B. Eyring

Experience:

"In 1977, I was serving as a full-time missionary in Cusco, Peru. My companion and I received approval to take all the missionaries in the Cusco zone to the magnificent Machu Picchu ruins.

Towards the end of our visit to the ruins, some of the missionaries wanted to go to the Inca Bridge, part of a mountain trail. Immediately, I felt in my heart the Spirit constraining me not to go there. The trail was on the side of a mountain with a 2,000-foot (610 m) drop-off. In several areas the trail was only wide enough for one person to pass at a time. My companion and I told them that we should not go to the Inca Bridge.

However, the missionaries insisted that we go. The pleadings became more intense, and despite what the Spirit had indicated to me, I gave in to the peer pressure and told them that we would visit the bridge but only if we were very careful.

We entered the trail that leads to the Inca Bridge with me at the end of the group, and at first everyone walked slowly, as agreed. Then the missionaries started to walk very fast and even run. They ignored my petitions to slow down. I felt obligated to catch up to them, to tell them that we had to turn back. I was far behind them, and I had to run fast to catch up with them.

As I came around a turn, in a passage too narrow for two to walk, I found a missionary standing still with his back against the rocks. I asked him why he was standing there. He told me he had received an impression to remain in that spot for a moment and that I should go on.

I felt the urgency to catch up to those ahead of us, so he helped me to pass him, and I was able to get a little farther down the trail. I noticed that the ground was full of greenery. I planted my right foot on the ground, realizing, as I fell, that there was no ground underneath the greenery. I desperately grabbed onto some branches that were underneath the trail. For a moment I could see down, some 2,000 feet below me, the Urubamba River, which crosses the Sacred Valley of the Incas. I felt as if my strength had left me, and it was only a matter of time before I could not hold on anymore. In that moment, I prayed intensely. It was a very brief prayer. I opened my mouth and said, "Father, help me!"

The branches were not strong enough to support the weight of my body. I knew the end was near. In the *very* moment when I was about to fall, I felt a firm hand take me by the arm and pull me up. With that help I was able to continue fighting and get myself back on the trail. The missionary who had stayed behind was the one who saved me.

But in reality our Father in Heaven saved me. He listened to my voice. I had heard the voice of the Spirit three times before, telling me not to go to the Inca Bridge, but I had not obeyed that voice. I was in shock, I was pale, and I did not know what to say. Then I remembered that the other missionaries were ahead of us, and so we went looking for them until we found them and told them what had happened to me.

We returned to Machu Picchu very carefully and in silence. On the return trip I remained silent, and the idea came to my mind that He had paid attention to my voice but that I had not paid any attention to His. There was a deep pain in my heart for disobeying His voice and at the same time a deep sense of gratitude for His mercy. He did not exercise His justice upon me, but in His great mercy, He had saved my life."
~Elder Juan A. Uceda

Scripture:

"Pray always, that you may come off conqueror; yea, that you may conquer Satan, and that you may escape the hands of the servants of Satan that do uphold his work."
~Doctrine and Covenants 10:5

Testimony:

"I hope as you have listened this morning that the Spirit has impressed on your minds and hearts something that you might do to have your questions answered or to find an inspired solution to the problem you face. I bear a solemn witness that Jesus is the Christ. Turn to Him and your prayers will be answered. In the name of Jesus Christ, amen."
~Elder James B. Martino   October 2015

Quest #16
Agency

Quote:

"Choice is an element of human dignity. Without the power of choice, a man is a lot less than a man. Without the exercise of choice a man never discovers what he can be or what he can do. Choice is the key to the future."

~George E. Farling

Experience:

"When I was a young lawyer in the San Francisco Bay Area, our firm did some legal work for the company that produced the Charlie Brown holiday TV specials. I became a fan of Charles Schulz and his creation — Peanuts, with Charlie Brown, Lucy, Snoopy, and other wonderful characters.

One of my favorite comic strips involved Lucy. As I remember it, Charlie Brown's baseball team was in an important game — Lucy was playing right field, and a high fly ball was hit to her. The bases were loaded, and it was the last of the ninth inning. If Lucy caught the ball, her team would win. If Lucy dropped the ball, the other team would win.

As could happen only in a comic strip, the entire team surrounded Lucy as the ball came down. Lucy was thinking, "If I catch the ball, I will be the hero; if I don't, I will be the goat."

The ball came down, and as her teammates eagerly looked on, Lucy dropped the ball. Charlie Brown threw his glove to the ground in disgust. Lucy then looked at her teammates, put her hands on her hips, and said, "How do you expect me to catch the ball when I am worried about our country's foreign policy?"

This was one of many fly balls Lucy dropped through the years, and she had a new excuse each time. While always humorous, Lucy's excuses were rationalizations; they were untrue reasons for her failure to catch the ball.

During the ministry of President Thomas S. Monson, he has often taught that decisions determine destiny. In that spirit my counsel tonight is to rise above any rationalizations that prevent us from making righteous decisions, especially with respect to serving Jesus Christ. In Isaiah we are taught we must "refuse the evil, and choose the good."

~ Elder Quentin L. Cook   October 2014

Scripture:

"And the Messiah cometh in the fulness of time, that he may redeem the children of men from the fall. And because that they are redeemed from the fall they have become free forever, knowing good from evil; to act for themselves and not to be acted upon, save it be by the punishment of the law at the great and last day, according to the commandments which God hath given.

Wherefore, men are free according to the flesh; and all things are given them which are expedient unto man. And they are free to choose liberty and eternal life, through the great Mediator of all men, or to choose captivity and death, according to the captivity and power of the devil; for he seeketh that all men might be miserable like unto himself."

~2 Nephi: 2:26–27

Testimony:

"My beloved brothers and sisters, don't walk! Run! Run to receive the blessings of agency by following the Holy Ghost and exercising the freedoms God has given us to do His will.

I bear my special witness on this special Easter day that Jesus Christ used His agency to do our Father's will.

Of our Savior, we sing, "His precious blood he freely spilt; His life he freely gave." And because He did, we have the priceless opportunity "to choose liberty and eternal life" through the power and blessings of His Atonement. May we freely choose to follow Him today and always, I pray in His holy name, even Jesus Christ, amen."

~ Elder Robert D. Hales   April 2015

Quest #17
Discipleship

Quote:

"How could it ever be possible that we of all people would not be excited about attending our Church worship services? Or get tired of reading the holy scriptures? I suppose this could be possible only if our hearts were past feeling to experience gratitude and awe for the sacred and sublime gifts God has granted us. Life-changing truths are before our eyes and at our fingertips, but sometimes we sleepwalk on the path of discipleship."

~Dieter F. Uchtdorf

Experience:

"In my family's pioneer history there are many accounts of noble souls who demonstrated the traits of true discipleship. My children's great-grandfather was a valiant disciple of Jesus Christ. His family were wealthy landowners in Denmark. As the favored son, he was to inherit the land of his father. He fell in love with a beautiful young woman who was not of the same social standing as his family. He was encouraged not to pursue the relationship. He was not inclined to follow his family's counsel, and on one of his visits to see her he discovered that all of her family had joined the Church. He refused to listen to the doctrine her family had embraced and forcefully told her that she had to choose between him and the Church. She boldly declared that she would not give up her religion.

With that forceful pronouncement, he decided he should listen to the teachings that were so important to her. Soon after, he was touched by the Spirit and he, too, became converted to the gospel. But when he informed his parents of his decision to join the Church and marry this young woman, they were angry with him and forced him to decide between his family and their wealth and the Church. He walked away from the comforts he had known all of his life, joined the Church, and married her.

Immediately, they started to prepare to leave Denmark and journey to Zion. Now without the support of his family, he had to work hard at any employment he could find to save for the journey to the new land. After a year of hard labor, he had saved enough for their passage. As soon as they were prepared to leave, their branch president came to them and said there was a family with greater need than he and his wife. He was asked to give up what he had saved so the needy family could go to Zion.

Discipleship requires sacrifice. They gave up their savings to the needy family, and then they began another year of hard labor to save to finance their journey. Eventually they arrived in Zion, but not before they had made many more sacrifices, showing true discipleship."
~Elder L. Tom Perry

Scripture:
"Therefore I would that ye should be perfect even as I, or your Father who is in heaven is perfect."
~3 Ne. 12:48

Testimony:
"Brothers and sisters, we are all called to be disciples of our Savior. Let this conference be your opportunity to "begin as in times of old, and come unto [Him] with all your heart." This is His Church. I bear my special witness that He lives. May He bless us in our eternal quest to become devoted and valiant disciples. In the name of Jesus Christ, amen."
~Elder Robert D. Hales   April 2017

Quest #18
Book of Mormon

Quote:

"There are three ways in which the Book of Mormon is the keystone of our religion. It is the keystone in our witness of Christ. It is the keystone of our doctrine. It is the keystone of testimony."
~*President Ezra Taft Benson   October 1986*

"There is a power in the book which will begin to flow into your lives the moment you begin a serious study of the book. You will find greater power to resist temptation. You will find the power to avoid deception. You will find the power to stay on the strait and narrow path."
~*President Ezra Taft Benson   October 1986*

Experience:

"On June 14, 1989, due to some misinformation about the Church, the government of Ghana banned all activities of The Church of Jesus Christ of Latter-day Saints within that African country. The government seized all Church property, and all missionary activity stopped. The members of the Church, who refer to this period as "the freeze," did their best to live the gospel without branch meetings or the support of missionaries. There are many inspiring stories about how the members kept the light of the gospel shining by worshipping in their homes and looking after each other as home and visiting teachers.

Eventually the misunderstanding was resolved, and on November 30, 1990, the freeze ended and normal Church activities resumed.1 Since then there has been an excellent relationship between the Church and the government of Ghana.

Members who lived through the freeze are quick to point out the blessings that came from that unusual period. The faith of many was strengthened through the adversity that they faced. But one blessing of the freeze came in an unusual way.

Nicholas Ofosu-Hene was a young policeman assigned to guard an LDS meetinghouse during the freeze. His duty was to watch over the building at night. When Nicholas first arrived at the meetinghouse, he saw that things had been scattered around, with papers, books, and furniture in disarray. In the midst of this disorder, he saw a copy of the Book of Mormon. He tried ignoring the book because he had been told that it was evil. But he felt strangely attracted to it. Finally, Nicholas could ignore the book no longer. He picked it up. He felt impelled to start reading it. He read through the night, tears running down his cheeks as he read.

The first time he picked it up, he read all of 1 Nephi. The second time, he read all of 2 Nephi. When he got to 2 Nephi chapter 25, he read the following: "And we talk of Christ, we rejoice in Christ, we preach of Christ, we prophesy of Christ, and we write according to our prophecies, that our children may know to what source they may look for a remission of their sins."

At that point, Nicholas felt the Spirit so strongly that he started sobbing. He realized that in the course of his reading he had received several spiritual promptings that this book was scripture, the most correct he had ever read. He realized that the Latter-day Saints, contrary to what he had heard, strongly believe in Jesus Christ. After the freeze ended and missionaries returned to Ghana, Nicholas, his wife, and his children joined the Church. When I saw him last year, he was a police commander and was serving as the president of the Tamale Ghana District of the Church. He says: "The Church has transformed my life. ... I thank the Almighty God for leading me into this gospel."
~Elder LeGrand R. Curtis Jr.

Scripture:

"And after having received the record of the Nephites, yea, even my servant Joseph Smith, Jun., might have power to translate through the mercy of God, by the power of God, the Book of Mormon.

And also those to whom these commandments were given, might have power to lay the foundation of this church, and to bring it forth out of obscurity and out of darkness, the only true and living church upon the face of the whole earth, with which I, the Lord, am well pleased, speaking unto the church collectively and not individually."
~Doctrine and Covenants 1:29-30

Testimony:

"Within the book's pages, you will discover the infinite love and incomprehensible grace of God. As you strive to follow the teachings you find there, your joy will expand, your understanding will increase, and the answers you seek to the many challenges mortality presents will be opened to you. As you look to the book, you look to the Lord. The Book of Mormon is the revealed word of God. Of this I testify, with all my heart and soul. In the name of Jesus Christ, amen.
~Elder Gary Stevenson   October 2016

Quest #19
Doctrine of Christ

Quote:
"The fundamental principles of our religion are the testimony of the Apostles and Prophets, concerning Jesus Christ, that He died, was buried, and rose again the third day, and ascended into heaven; and all other things which pertain to our religion are only appendages to it."
~Joseph Smith

Experience:
"At the same time it should be remembered that not every statement made by a Church leader, past or present, necessarily constitutes doctrine. It is commonly understood in the Church that a statement made by one leader on a single occasion often represents a personal, though well-considered, opinion, not meant to be official or binding for the whole Church. The Prophet Joseph Smith taught that "a prophet [is] a prophet only when he [is] acting as such."
President J. Reuben Clark, observed:

"To this point runs a simple story my father told me as a boy, I do not know on what authority, but it illustrates the point. His story was that during the excitement incident to the coming of [Johnston's] Army, Brother Brigham preached to the people in a morning meeting a sermon vibrant with defiance to the approaching army, and declaring an intention to oppose and drive them back. In the afternoon meeting he arose and said that Brigham Young had been talking in the morning, but the Lord was going to talk now. He then delivered an address, the tempo of which was the opposite from the morning talk. ...

"... The Church will know by the testimony of the Holy Ghost in the body of the members, whether the brethren in voicing their views are 'moved upon by the Holy Ghost'; and in due time that knowledge will be made manifest."
~Elder D. Todd Christofferson   April 2012

Scripture:
"This is my doctrine, and it is the doctrine which the Father hath given unto me; and I bear record of the Father, and the Father beareth record of me, and the Holy Ghost beareth record of the Father and me; and I bear record that the Father commandeth all men, everywhere, to repent and believe in me.

"And whoso believeth in me, and is baptized, the same shall be saved; and they are they who shall inherit the kingdom of God.

"And whoso believeth not in me, and is not baptized, shall be damned.

"… And whoso believeth in me believeth in the Father also; and unto him will the Father bear record of me, for he will visit him with fire and with the Holy Ghost. …

"Verily, verily, I say unto you, that this is my doctrine, and whoso buildeth upon this buildeth upon my rock, and the gates of hell shall not prevail against them"
~3 Nephi 11:32–35, 39

Testimony:

"As our Easter celebration approaches, I express my own witness that Jesus of Nazareth was and is the Son of God, the very Messiah of ancient prophecy. He is the Christ, who suffered in Gethsemane, died on the cross, was buried, and who indeed rose again the third day. He is the resurrected Lord, through whom we shall all be resurrected and by whom all who will may be redeemed and exalted in His heavenly kingdom. This is our doctrine, confirming all prior testaments of Jesus Christ and stated anew for our own time. In the name of Jesus Christ, amen."
~Elder D. Todd Christofferson   April 2012

Quest #20
Service

Quote:

"Loving service and devotion to the needs of others was perhaps the chief characteristic of the Savior's mortal life. It will always be a mark of the Master's disciples."

~Elder Jeffrey R. Holland

Experience:

"Last summer I met Sister Yvette Bugingo, who at age 11 fled from place to place after her father was killed and three of her brothers went missing in a war-torn part of the world. Yvette and the remaining family members eventually lived for six and a half years as refugees in a neighboring country until they were able to move to a permanent home, where they were blessed by a caring couple who helped with transportation, schools, and other things. She said they "were basically an answer to our prayers." Her beautiful mother and adorable little sister are with us tonight, singing in the choir. I have wondered many times since meeting these wonderful women, "What if their story were my story?"

As sisters we make up more than half of the Lord's storehouse to help Heavenly Father's children. His storehouse is not composed just of goods but also of time, talents, skills, and our divine nature. Sister Rosemary M. Wixom has taught, "The divine nature within us ignites our desire to reach out to others and prompts us to act."

~Linda K Burton   April 2016

Scripture:

"And behold, I tell you these things that ye may learn wisdom; that ye may learn that when ye are in the service of your fellow beings ye are only in the service of your God."

~Mosiah 2:17

Testimony:

"Heavenly Father hears and answers our prayers. I witness that we grow closer to the Savior as we, out of pure love, serve others for Him. I so leave you that sure witness in the name of Jesus Christ, amen."

~President Henry B. Eyring   April 2016

Quest #21
God's Love

Quote:

"If we wish to learn truly how to love, all we need to do is reflect on the life of our Savior. When we partake of the sacramental emblems, we are reminded of the greatest example of love in all the world's history. "For God so loved the world, that he gave his only begotten Son."

The Savior's love for us was so great that it caused "even God, the greatest of all, to tremble because of pain, and to bleed at every pore."

Because the Savior laid down His life for us, we have a brightness of hope, a confidence and security that when we pass from this worldly existence, we will live again with Him. Through the Atonement of Jesus Christ, we can be cleansed of sin and stand as partakers of the gift of our Almighty Father. Then we will know the glory that God "hath prepared for them that love him."

This is the transforming power of charity.

When Jesus gave His disciples a new commandment to "love one another; as I have loved you," He gave to them the grand key to happiness in this life and glory in the next."
~Elder Joseph P. Wirthlin   October 2007

Experience:

"As a young missionary I was assigned to a small island of about 700 inhabitants in a remote area of the South Pacific. To me the heat was oppressive, the mosquitoes were terrible, the mud was everywhere, the language was impossible, and the food was—well, "different."

After a few months our island was struck by a powerful hurricane. The devastation was massive. Crops were ruined, lives were lost, housing was blown away, and the telegraph station—our only link to the outside world—was destroyed. A small government boat normally came every month or two, so we rationed our food to last four or five weeks, hoping the boat would come. But no boat came. Every day we became weaker. There were acts of great kindness, but as the sixth and seventh weeks passed with very little food, our strength slipped noticeably. My native companion, Feki, helped me in every way he could, but as the eighth week commenced, I had no energy. I just sat under the shade of a tree and prayed and read scriptures and spent hours and hours pondering the things of eternity.

The ninth week began with little outward change. However, there was a great inward change. I felt the Lord's love more deeply than ever before and learned firsthand that His love "is the most desirable above all things ... yea, and the most joyous to the soul" (1 Ne. 11:22–23).

I was pretty much skin and bones by now. I remember watching, with deep reverence, my heart beating, my lungs breathing, and thinking what a marvelous body God has created to house our equally marvelous spirit! The thought of a permanent union of these two elements, made possible through the Savior's love, atoning sacrifice, and Resurrection, was so inspiring and satisfying that any physical discomfort faded into oblivion.

When we understand who God is, who we are, how He loves us, and what His plan is for us, fear evaporates. When we get the tiniest glimpse of these truths, our concern over worldly things vanishes. To think we actually fall for Satan's lies that power, fame, or wealth is important is truly laughable—or would be were it not so sad.

I learned that just as rockets must overcome the pull of gravity to roar into space, so we must overcome the pull of the world to soar into the eternal realms of understanding and love. I realized my mortal life might end there, but there was no panic. I knew life would continue, and whether here or there didn't really matter. What did matter was how much love I had in my heart. I knew I needed more! I knew that our joy now and forever is inextricably tied to our capacity to love.

As these thoughts filled and lifted my soul, I gradually became aware of some excited voices. My companion Feki's eyes were dancing as he said, "Kolipoki, a boat has arrived, and it is full of food. We are saved! Aren't you excited?" I wasn't sure, but since the boat had come, that must be God's answer, so yes, I was happy. Feki gave me some food and said, "Here, eat." I hesitated. I looked at the food. I looked at Feki. I looked into the sky and closed my eyes.

I felt something very deep. I was grateful my life here would go on as before; still, there was a wistful feeling—a subtle sense of postponement, as when darkness closes the brilliant colors of a perfect sunset and you realize you must wait for another evening to again enjoy such beauty."
~John H. Groberg   October 2004

Scripture:

"For God so loved the world, that he gave his only begotten Son, that whosoever believeth in him should not perish, but have everlasting life."
~John 3:16

Testimony:

"I know He lives. I know He loves us. I know we can feel His love here and now. I know His voice is one of perfect mildness which penetrates to our very center. I know He smiles and is filled with compassion and love. I know He is full of gentleness, kindness, mercy, and desire to help. I love Him with all my heart. I testify that when we are ready, His pure love instantly moves across time and space, reaches down, and pulls us up from the depths of any tumultuous sea of darkness, sin, sorrow, death, or despair we may find ourselves in and brings us into the light and life and love of eternity. In the name of Jesus Christ, amen."

~*John H. Groberg   October 2004*

Quest #22
Faith

Quote:

"Faith in Jesus Christ is a gift from heaven that comes as we choose to believe and as we seek it and hold on to it. Your faith is either growing stronger or becoming weaker. Faith is a principle of power, important not only in this life but also in our progression beyond the veil. By the grace of Christ, we will one day be saved through faith on His name. The future of your faith is not by chance, but by choice."

~Elder Neil L. Andersen   October 2015

Experience:

"An experience I had when I was 15 years old was foundational for me. My faithful mother had valiantly tried to help me establish the foundations of faith in my life. I attended sacrament meeting, Primary, then Young Men and seminary. I had read the Book of Mormon and had always prayed individually. At that time a dramatic event occurred in our family when my beloved older brother was considering a potential mission call. My wonderful father, a less-active Church member, wanted him to continue his education and not serve a mission. This became a point of contention.

In a remarkable discussion with my brother, who was five years older and led the discussion, we concluded that his decision on whether to serve a mission depended on three issues:

(1) Was Jesus Christ divine?
(2) Was the Book of Mormon true?
(3) Was Joseph Smith the prophet of the Restoration?

As I prayed sincerely that night, the Spirit confirmed to me the truth of all three questions. I also came to understand that almost every decision I would make for the rest of my life would be based on the answers to those three questions. I particularly realized that faith in the Lord Jesus Christ was essential. In looking back, I recognize that, primarily because of my mother, the foundations were in place for me to receive the spiritual confirmation that evening. My brother, who already had a testimony, made the decision to serve a mission and ultimately won our father's support.

~Elder Quentin L. Cook   April 2017

Scripture:

"Then said Jesus unto the twelve, Will ye also go away?

"Then Simon Peter answered him, Lord, to whom shall we go? thou hast the words of eternal life.

"And we believe and are sure that thou art that Christ, the Son of the living God."

~John 6:66–69

Testimony:

"I am grateful for the fortification of the foundations of faith that has come from this conference. My plea is that we will make the sacrifices and have the humility necessary to strengthen the foundations of our faith in the Lord Jesus Christ. Of Him I bear my sure witness in the name of Jesus Christ, amen."

~Elder Quentin L. Cook   April 2017

Quest #23
Sabbath

Quote:

"President David O. McKay called attention to another most important phase of this subject. He said that the Christian Sabbath of course is Sunday, in commemoration of the resurrection of the Savior on the first day of the week. He calls the resurrection of Christ the greatest event in all history and notes that by proper observance of the Sabbath we show our respect for the Lord's passion and his resurrection from the dead. (See Gospel Ideals, Deseret News Press, 1953, pp. 397–98.)

With this thought in mind, let us ask ourselves how important the Lord's atonement is to us. How dear to us is the Lord Jesus Christ? How deeply are we concerned about immortality? Is the resurrection of vital interest to us?

We can readily see that observance of the Sabbath is an indication of the depth of our conversion."

~Elder Mark E. Petersen   April 1975

Experience:

"My brothers and sisters and friends, for some time I have pondered what I might speak about today. I seem to have been led in my thinking by a concern that so many in our generation are missing great blessings by not honoring the Lord's day.

I confess that as a young boy, Sunday was not my favorite day. Grandfather shut down the action. We didn't have any transportation. We couldn't drive the car. He wouldn't even let us start the motor. We couldn't ride the horses, or the steers, or the sheep. It was the Sabbath, and by commandment, the animals also needed rest. We walked to Church and everywhere else we wanted to go. I can honestly say that we observed both the spirit and the letter of Sabbath worship.

By today's standards, perhaps Grandfather's interpretation of Sabbath day activities seems extreme, but something wonderful has been lost in our lives. To this day, I have been pondering to try to understand fully what has slipped away. Part of it was knowing that I was well on the Lord's side of the line. Another part was the feeling that Satan's influence was farther away. Mostly it was the reinforcement received by the spiritual power which was generated. We had the rich feeling that the spiritual "fulness of the earth" (D&C 59:16) was ours, as promised by the Lord in section 59 of the Doctrine and Covenants."

~President James E. Faust   October 1991

Scripture:

"And that thou mayest more fully keep thyself unspotted from the world, thou shalt go to the house of prayer and offer up thy sacraments upon my holy day;

For verily this is a day appointed unto you to rest from your labors, and to pay thy devotions unto the Most High;

Nevertheless thy vows shall be offered up in righteousness on all days and at all times;

But remember that on this, the Lord's day, thou shalt offer thine oblations and thy sacraments unto the Most High, confessing thy sins unto thy brethren, and before the Lord."

~Doctrine and Covenants 59:9-12

Testimony:

" I bear you testimony that to properly observe the Lord's holy day is one of the most important things we can ever do. It is an essential step toward our eternal salvation.

I do not believe we will be saved if we constantly violate the Sabbath and fling our disobedience into the face of the very God we hope will save us.

How dare we trifle with the Sabbath day?

How dare we trifle with Almighty God?

The Lord declares that to qualify to enter his presence we must live by every word that proceeds forth from his mouth (see D&C 84:44), and the law of the Sabbath is one of the most important in the entire gospel plan.

May we have the courage and the good sense to keep it, I humbly pray in the sacred name of Jesus Christ. Amen."

~Elder Mark E. Petersen   April 1975

Quest #24
Love

Quote:

He drew a circle that shut me out—
Heretic, rebel, a thing to flout.
But Love and I had the wit to win:
We drew a circle that took him in!
~Edwin Markham

Experience:

"Often our opportunities to show our love come unexpectedly. An example of such an opportunity appeared in a newspaper article in October 1981. So impressed was I with the love and compassion related therein that I have kept the clipping in my files for over 30 years.

The article indicates that an Alaska Airlines nonstop flight from Anchorage, Alaska, to Seattle, Washington—a flight carrying 150 passengers—was diverted to a remote Alaskan town in order to transport a gravely injured child. The two-year-old boy had severed an artery in his arm when he fell on a piece of glass while playing near his home. The town was 450 miles (725 km) south of Anchorage and was certainly not on the flight path. However, medics at the scene had sent out a frantic request for help, and so the flight was diverted to pick up the child and take him to Seattle so that he could be treated in a hospital.

When the flight touched down near the remote town, medics informed the pilot that the boy was bleeding so badly he could not survive the flight to Seattle. A decision was made to fly another 200 miles (320 km) out of the way to Juneau, Alaska, the nearest city with a hospital.

After transporting the boy to Juneau, the flight headed for Seattle, now hours behind schedule. Not one passenger complained, even though most of them would miss appointments and connecting flights. In fact, as the minutes and hours ticked by, they took up a collection, raising a considerable sum for the boy and his family.

As the flight was about to land in Seattle, the passengers broke into a cheer when the pilot announced that he had received word by radio that the boy was going to be all right."

~President Thomas S. Monson   April 2014

Scripture:

"A new commandment I give unto you, That ye love one another; as I have loved you, that ye also love one another."

~John 13:34

Testimony:

"Beyond comprehension, my brothers and sisters, is the love of God for us. Because of this love, He sent His Son, who loved us enough to give His life for us, that we might have eternal life. As we come to understand this incomparable gift, our hearts will be filled with love for our Eternal Father, for our Savior, and for all mankind. That such may be so is my earnest prayer in the sacred name of Jesus Christ, amen."

~President Thomas S. Monson

Quest #25
Happiness

Quote:

"What I am suggesting and asking is that we turn from the negativism that so permeates our society and look for the remarkable good in the land and times in which we live, that we speak of one another's virtues more than we speak of one another's faults, that optimism replace pessimism. Let our faith replace our fears."

~*President Gordon B. Hinckley*

Experience:

"Late one evening on a Pacific isle, a small boat slipped silently to its berth at the crude pier. Two Polynesian women helped Meli Mulipola from the boat and guided him to the well-worn pathway leading to the village road. The women marveled at the bright stars, which twinkled in the midnight sky. The moonlight guided them along their way. However, Meli Mulipola could not appreciate these delights of nature—the moon, the stars, the sky—for he was blind.

Brother Mulipola's vision had been normal until a fateful day when, while working on a pineapple plantation, light turned suddenly to darkness and day became perpetual night. He was depressed and despondent until he learned the good news of the gospel of Jesus Christ. His life was brought into compliance with the teachings of the Church, and he once again felt hope and joy.

Brother Mulipola and his loved ones had made a long voyage, having learned that one who held the priesthood of God was visiting among the islands of the Pacific. He sought a blessing, and it was my privilege, along with another who held the Melchizedek Priesthood, to provide that blessing to him. As we finished, I noted that tears were streaming from his sightless eyes, coursing down his brown cheeks and tumbling finally upon his native dress. He dropped to his knees and prayed: "O God, Thou knowest I am blind. Thy servants have blessed me that my sight might return. Whether in Thy wisdom I see light or whether I see darkness all the days of my life, I will be eternally grateful for the truth of Thy gospel, which I now see and which provides the light of my life."

He rose to his feet and, smiling, thanked us for providing the blessing. He then disappeared into the still of the night. Silently he came; silently he departed. But his presence I shall never forget. I reflected upon the

message of the Master: "I am the light of the world: he that followeth me shall not walk in darkness, but shall have the light of life."
~*President Thomas S. Monson   April 2009*

Scripture:

"Adam fell that men might be; and men are, that they might have joy."
~*2 Nephi 2:25*

Testimony:

"Heed these words of the Psalmist: "I have set the Lord always before me: because he is at my right hand, I shall not be moved. ... In [His] presence is fulness of joy." As this principle is embedded in our hearts, each and every day can be a day of joy and gladness. I so testify in the sacred name of Jesus Christ, amen."
~*President Russell M. Nelson   October 2016*

Quest #26
Endure

Quote:

"No matter how serious the trial, how deep the distress, how great the affliction, [God] will never desert us. He never has, and He never will. He cannot do it. It is not His character [to do so]. ... He will [always] stand by us. We may pass through the fiery furnace; we may pass through deep waters; but we shall not be consumed nor overwhelmed. We shall emerge from all these trials and difficulties the better and purer for them."
~President George Q. Cannon

Experience:

"In 1968 a marathon runner by the name of John Stephen Akhwari represented Tanzania in an international competition. "A little over an hour after [the winner] had crossed the finish line, John Stephen Akhwari ... approached the stadium, the last man to complete the journey. [Though suffering from fatigue, leg cramps, dehydration, and disorientation,] a voice called from within to go on, and so he went on. Afterwards, it was written, 'Today we have seen a young African runner who symbolizes the finest in human spirit, a performance that gives meaning to the word courage.' For some, the only reward is a personal one. [There are no medals, only] the knowledge that they finished what they set out to do" (*The Last African Runner, Olympiad Series, written, directed, and produced by Bud Greenspan, Cappy Productions, 1976, videocassette*). When asked why he would complete a race he could never win, Akhwari replied, "My country did not send me 5,000 miles to start the race; my country sent me to finish the race."
~Elder Robert D. Hales   April 1998

Scripture:

"And ye shall be hated of all men for my name's sake: but he that shall endure unto the end, the same shall be saved."
~ *Mark 13:13*

"My son, peace be unto thy soul; thine adversity and thine afflictions shall be but a small moment;
And then, if thou endure it well, God shall exalt thee on high; thou shalt triumph over all thy foes."
~*D&C 121: 7-8*

"And, if you keep my commandments and endure to the end you shall have eternal life, which gift is the greatest of all the gifts of God."
~*D&C 14: 7*

<u>Testimony:</u>

"There is nothing that we are enduring that Jesus does not understand, and He waits for us to go to our Heavenly Father in prayer. I testify that if we will be obedient and if we are diligent, our prayers will be answered, our problems will diminish, our fears will dissipate, light will come upon us, the darkness of despair will be dispersed, and we will be close to the Lord and feel of His love and of the comfort of the Holy Ghost. It is my prayer that we can find the faith, courage, and strength to endure to the end so that we may feel the joy of faithfully returning to the arms of our Heavenly Father, in the name of Jesus Christ, amen."

~*Elder Robert D. Hales   April 1998*

Quest #27
Integrity

Quote:

"It is difficult for a person to display virtuous traits if he or she lacks integrity. Without integrity, honesty is often forgotten. If integrity is absent, civility is impaired. If integrity is not important, spirituality is difficult to maintain."

~Bishop H. David Burton   October 2009

Experience:

"During World War II, President James E. Faust, then a young enlisted man in the United States Army, applied for officer candidate school. He appeared before a board of inquiry composed of what he described as "hard-bitten career soldier[s]." After a while their questions turned to matters of religion. The final questions were these:

"In times of war should not the moral code be relaxed? Does not the stress of battle justify men in doing things that they would not do when at home under normal situations?"

President Faust relates:

"I recognized that here was a chance perhaps to make some points and look broad-minded. I knew perfectly well that the men who were asking me this question did not live by the standards that I had been taught. The thought flashed through my mind that perhaps I could say that I had my own beliefs but did not wish to impose them on others. But there seemed to flash before my mind the faces of the many people to whom I had taught the law of chastity as a missionary. In the end I simply said, 'I do not believe there is a double standard of morality.'

"I left the hearing resigned to the fact that [they] would not like the answers I had given ... and would surely score me very low. A few days later when the scores were posted, to my astonishment I had passed. I was in the first group taken for officer's candidate school! ...

"This was one of the critical crossroads of my life."

Scripture:

"Let virtue garnish thy thoughts unceasingly; then shall thy confidence wax strong in the presence of God"

~D&C 121:45

Testimony:

"When we are true to the sacred principles of honesty and integrity, we are true to our faith, and we are true to ourselves.

My prayer is that as Latter-day Saints we will be known as among the most honest people in the world. And it might be said of us as it was of the people of Anti-Nephi-Lehi that we are "perfectly honest and upright in all things; and ... firm in the faith of Christ, even unto the end" (Alma 27:27). In the name of Jesus Christ, amen."

~ *Richard C. Edgley, First Counselor in the Presiding Bishopric*   *October 2006*

Quest #28
Temples

Quote:
"Until you have entered the house of the Lord and have received all the blessings which await you there, you have not obtained everything the Church has to offer. The all-important and crowning blessings of membership in the Church are those blessings which we receive in the temples of God."

~President Thomas S. Monson   April 2011

Experience:
"In 1976, when we were living in Costa Rica, the mission president asked my husband to help organize the first trip from the mission to a temple. The Central America Mission then included Costa Rica, Panama, Nicaragua, and Honduras. The closest temple was the Mesa Arizona Temple. The trip required us to travel five days each way, crossing six borders. The financial sacrifice for most of those who went was great. They sold their television sets, bikes, skates, and anything else they could sell. We traveled in two uncomfortable buses day and night. Some of the members had used all their money to pay for the bus fare and had taken only crackers and margarine to eat on the way.

"Why do members of the Church so willingly and happily make such great sacrifices to go to the temple?

"I have never forgotten the great outpouring of the Spirit we experienced during the three days we spent at the Mesa Temple. I was deeply touched as I watched family members embrace each other with tears streaming down their faces after being sealed for the eternities."

~ Silvia H. Allred, First Counselor in the Relief Society General Presidency October 2008

Scripture:
"Organize yourselves; prepare every needful thing; and establish a house, even a house of prayer, a house of fasting, a house of faith, a house of learning, a house of glory, a house of order, a house of God;"

~D&C 88:119

Testimony:
"Brothers and sisters, I pray that each of us will honor the Savior and make any necessary changes to see ourselves in His sacred temples. In doing so, we can accomplish His holy purposes and prepare ourselves and our families for all the blessings the Lord and His Church can bestow in

this life and eternity. I bear my sure witness that the Savior lives. In the name of Jesus Christ, amen.

~Elder Quentin L. CooK   April 2016

Quest #29
Patience

Quote:

"No man is himself in acute sorrow. No man is himself in anger. No man is himself with feelings of offense. And decisions that will wait are safer with waiting – waiting for time to take over, for the dust to clear away, for tempers to cool, for perspective to return, for the real issues to show themselves, for the real values to reappear, for judgement to emerge and mature.

We should think seriously before we slam doors, before we burn bridges, before we saw off the limb on which we find ourselves sitting. Decisions in acute sorrow, decisions in anger, decisions under pressure, decisions that haven't been thought through are less likely to be mature and safe decisions."
~Elder Richard L. Evans

If the way be full of trial; Weary not!
If it's one of sore denial, Weary not!
If it now be one of weeping,
There will come a joyous greeting,
When the harvest we are reaping—Weary not!

Do not weary by the way,
Whatever be thy lot;
There awaits a brighter day
To all, to all who weary not!
~"If the Way Be Full of Trial, Weary Not," Deseret Sunday School Songs, 1909, no. 158.

Experience:

"In the 1960s, a professor at Stanford University began a modest experiment testing the willpower of four-year-old children. He placed before them a large marshmallow and then told them they could eat it right away or, if they waited for 15 minutes, they could have two marshmallows.

He then left the children alone and watched what happened behind a two-way mirror. Some of the children ate the marshmallow immediately; some could wait only a few minutes before giving in to temptation. Only 30 percent were able to wait.

It was a mildly interesting experiment, and the professor moved on to other areas of research, for, in his own words, "there are only so many things you can do with kids trying not to eat marshmallows." But as time went on, he kept track of the children and began to notice an interesting correlation: the children who could not wait struggled later in life and had more behavioral problems, while those who waited tended to be more positive and better motivated, have higher grades and incomes, and have healthier relationships.

What started as a simple experiment with children and marshmallows became a landmark study suggesting that the ability to wait▯—to be patient▯—was a key character trait that might predict later success in life."

~President Dieter F. Uchtdorf   April 2010

Scripture:

"Be patient in afflictions, for thou shalt have many; but endure them, for, lo, I am with thee, even unto the end of thy days."

~D&C 24:8

Testimony:

"God does live and He does fulfill His promises, and to the many testimonies given, I wish to add mine. I know that even in times of affliction and tribulation, if we patiently endure in faith, blessings of comfort and hope will come into our lives, and we will be able to partake of that "incomprehensible joy" of which Ammon and his brothers received. (See Alma 27:17–18; Alma 28:8.)

Therefore, in the words of Joseph Smith, "Stand fast, ye Saints of God, hold on a little while longer, and the storm of life will be past, and you will be rewarded by that God whose servants you are, and who will duly appreciate all your toils and afflictions for Christ's sake and the Gospel's." (Teachings of the Prophet Joseph Smith, p. 185.)

These things I say in the name of Jesus Christ, amen."

~Elder Angel Abrea   April 1992

Quest #30
Friendship

Quote:

No man is an island;
No man stands alone.
Each man's joy is a joy to me;
Each man's grief is my own.
We need one another,
So I will defend
Each man as my brother;
Each man as my friend.
~John Donne

"If we truly want to be tools in the hands of our Heavenly Father in bringing to pass His eternal purposes, we need only to be a friend."
~Marlin K. Jensen, of the Presidency of the Seventy, April 1999

Experience:

"The north coast of California is home to the world's tallest trees. A walk through a virgin old-growth redwood forest can be one of the most awe-inspiring experiences you'll ever have. These trees sometimes live to be over 2,000 years old and can reach heights of 300 feet and more. The tallest redwood tree ever recorded was 367 feet in height. That is taller than a football field and about one-third again as tall as the Salt Lake Temple. The gigantic redwoods dwarf their other softwood and hardwood neighbors, thus becoming "the Mount Everest of all living things."

The coastal redwoods are truly lords of their realm and a most exquisite creation of our Father in Heaven. They reign over associated trees because of their overwhelming height and majestic beauty. However, there is another feature of these towering giants that is truly remarkable and somewhat unknown to most of us. Even though they grow up to heights of 300 feet and can weigh more than one million pounds, these trees have a very shallow root system. Their roots only go down three to six feet but can spread out several hundred feet. As these roots extend out, they intertwine with their brother and sister redwoods and other trees as well. This intertwining of roots creates a webbing effect. Most engineers would tell you this shallow root system still would be impossible to keep the redwoods intact and protected against strong winds and floods. However, the interconnecting root systems are the secret of their strength and teach us a great lesson.

First, let's acknowledge that these magnificent giants simply could not make it alone. Without being connected to other family members and helpful neighbors, they would not survive."

~ *Richard H. Winkel, Of the Second Quorum of the Seventy,   October Conference 1999*

Scripture:

"And it came to pass that he said unto them: Behold, here are the waters of Mormon (for thus were they called) and now, as ye are desirous to come into the fold of God, and to be called his people, and are willing to bear one another's burdens, that they may be light;

Yea, and are willing to mourn with those that mourn; yea, and comfort those that stand in need of comfort, and to stand as witnesses of God at all times and in all things, and in all places that ye may be in, even until death, that ye may be redeemed of God, and be numbered with those of the first resurrection, that ye may have eternal life—

Now I say unto you, if this be the desire of your hearts, what have you against being baptized in the name of the Lord, as a witness before him that ye have entered into a covenant with him, that ye will serve him and keep his commandments, that he may pour out his Spirit more abundantly upon you?"

~*Mosiah 18: 8-10*

Testimony:

"May all who profess to be Christians, all who know and testify of Jesus, come unto Him and follow His teachings and example, being one as Heavenly Father and Jesus are one in purpose, to unite ourselves, to lift and strengthen each other, and take upon us one another's burdens as our Savior has taken our burdens upon Him, in the name of Jesus Christ, amen."

~*Elder Robert D. Hales   October 1997*

Reader,

So, you got to the end of my book. I hope that means you enjoyed it!

Whether or not you did, I would just like to thank you for giving me your valuable time to let us try to entertain you. I am truly blessed to have such a fulfilling occupation, but I only have that job because of people like you; people kind enough to give my books a chance and to spend their hard-earned money buying them. For that I am eternally grateful.

If you would like to find out more about my other books, then please visit my website for full details. You can find it at:

www.questcheney.com

Also feel free to contact me on Facebook, Twitter, Goodreads, or email (all of the details are available on the website), as I would love to hear from you.

LEAVE ME A REVIEW

If you enjoyed this book and would like to help, then you could think about leaving a review on Amazon, Goodreads, or anywhere else that readers visit. The most important part of how well a book sells is how many positive reviews it has, so if you leave me one then you are directly helping me to continue on my journey as a writer.

THANK YOU!

Thanks in advance to everyone who does this. It means a lot. I appreciate all of you who read my books and especially those who review them.

SIGN UP FOR MORE

If you would like more information about my books, or would like to be notified when my new books are being released,

Sign up on the website

About the Author

Jeff Cheney has worked as a civilian contract mechanic for the US Army, a heavy equipment mechanic, a High School teacher, and currently works in high technology computer chip manufacturing. He has been writing science fiction and fantasy stories for enjoyment for over thirty-five years and has published five SF novels with his brothers.

He enjoys coaching youth basketball, working on cars and doing woodworking when the time allows. He has three grown children and lives in a small town in NW Oregon with his wife of 32 years.

Jeff has served in a multitude of callings in the Church of Jesus Christ of Latter-day Saints over the years; as a missionary in Guayaquil, Ecuador as a young man, and many others as the years have gone by.

www.ingramcontent.com/pod-product-compliance
Lightning Source LLC
Chambersburg PA
CBHW071850020426
42331CB00007B/1936